INSECTS

Written and Illustrated by Beverly Armstrong

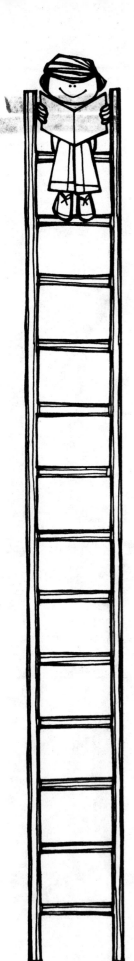

The
Learning
Works

Edited by Sherri M. Butterfield

The purchase of this book entitles the individual
classroom teacher to reproduce copies for use
in the classroom.

The reproduction of any part for an entire school
or school system or for commercial use is strictly
prohibited.

No form of this work may be reproduced or
transmitted or recorded without written permis-
sion from the publisher.

Write for information about our educational products.
The Learning Works • Box 6187, Dept. N • Santa Barbara, CA 93160

To the Teacher

INSECTS is a Learning Works mini-unit created especially for children in grades one through four. The purpose of this unit is to blend the presentation of facts about insects with the practice of essential skills to produce the very best in theme-related teaching and results-oriented learning.

Information about insects is presented in easy-to-read passages. Kids learn how insects live, move, eat, grow, and defend themselves. Associated activities involve children in observing and comparing, matching and classifying, identifying and labeling, counting and measuring, ordering and sequencing, recognizing letters and words, locating and using information, and following directions. These tasks are carefully designed to improve hand-eye coordination; increase skill in visual discrimination, word recognition, and spelling; stimulate curiosity; and foster creative expression.

In addition to information and activity sheets, this book includes a page of **awards**, patterns for **borders** to put finishing touches on classroom displays, and an **All-Purpose Page**. You can reproduce this bug-bordered sheet, fill it with announcements, art project ideas, math problems to be worked, or spelling words to be learned—and then reproduce it again so that you will have one for every member of your class. Or you can reproduce it as is and invite children to add content or use it for their own creative writing. The many illustrations throughout this book may be reproduced and used as **clip art** on bulletins, games, invitations, name tags, notes, and newsletters.

This mini-unit offers stimulating activities related to a high-interest subject so that young readers can strengthen their skill in essential areas while increasing their knowledge about insects.

Contents

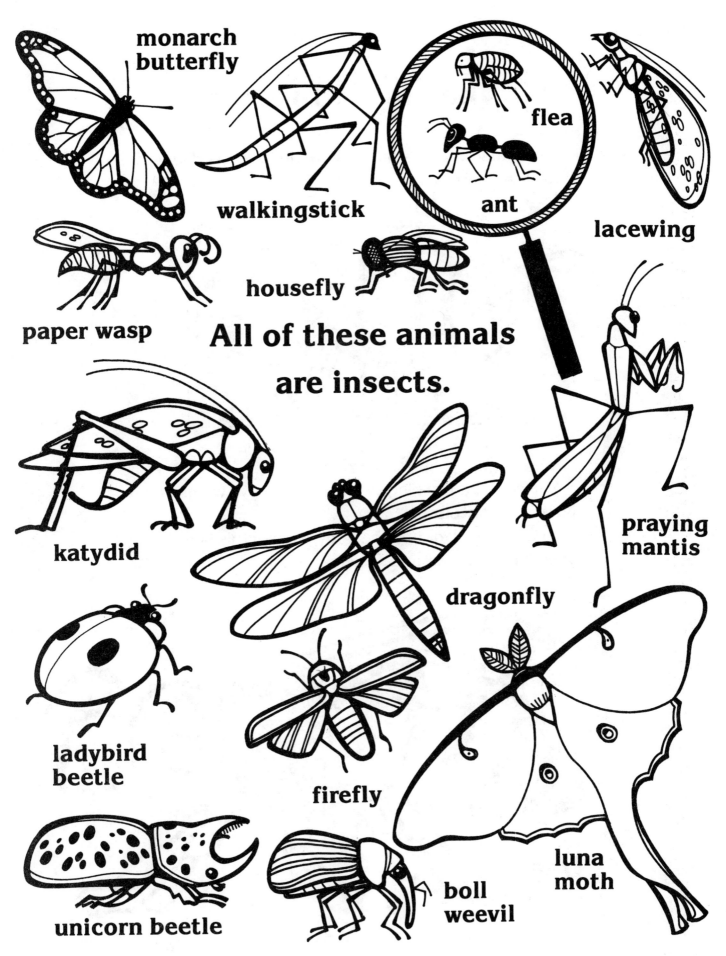

monarch butterfly

walkingstick

flea

ant

lacewing

paper wasp

housefly

All of these animals are insects.

katydid

dragonfly

praying mantis

ladybird beetle

firefly

luna moth

unicorn beetle

boll weevil

Name _____

What Is an Insect?

An **insect** is a small animal. Its body is divided into three parts.

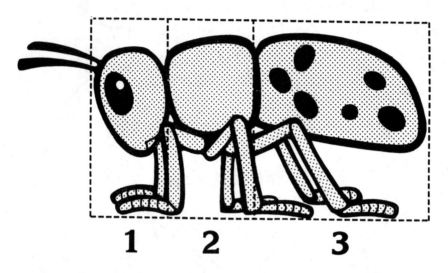

1   2   3

Insects have six legs. Most insects have wings and feelers, or **antennae**.

Count the legs and the body parts of this bee. Can you find its wings and feelers?

bee

Name _____

Which Ones Are Insects?

Some of these animals are insects, and some are not. Remember that an insect has six legs. Color the insects.

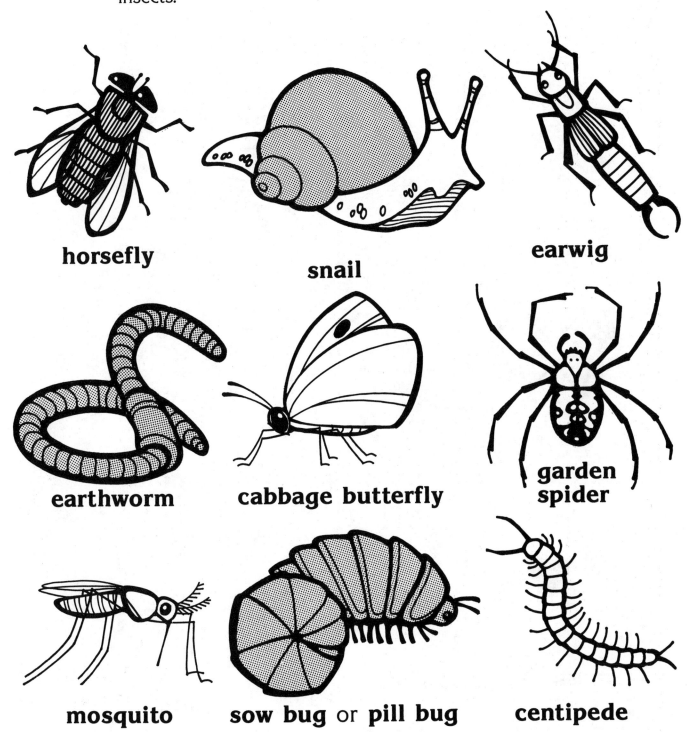

horsefly

snail

earwig

earthworm

cabbage butterfly

garden spider

mosquito

sow bug or **pill bug**

centipede

How Are Insects Grouped?

Scientists have divided insects into twenty-five groups, or **orders**. The insects in each group are alike in some ways. Here are some of the orders of insects.

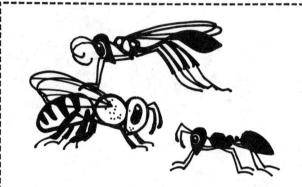

bees, wasps, and ants

beetles

butterflies and moths

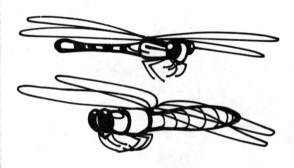

dragonflies

grasshoppers, crickets, and roaches

termites

Name _____

Connect the Insects

Draw a line to connect each pair of insects that
are from the same order.

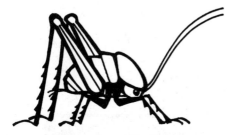

camel cricket

ten-spot dragonfly

red darter

potter wasp

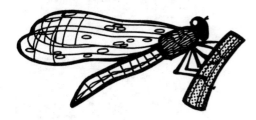

fire ant

buckeye butterfly

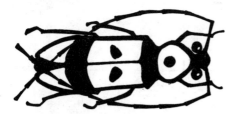

long-horned beetle

American grasshopper

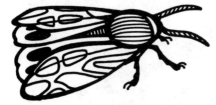

tiger moth

steel beetle

Name _____

Name Game

Can you write these insect names in the puzzle?
Look at the letters and count the squares to see where
each name fits.

ant   beetle   cricket   firefly
katydid   mosquito   wasp

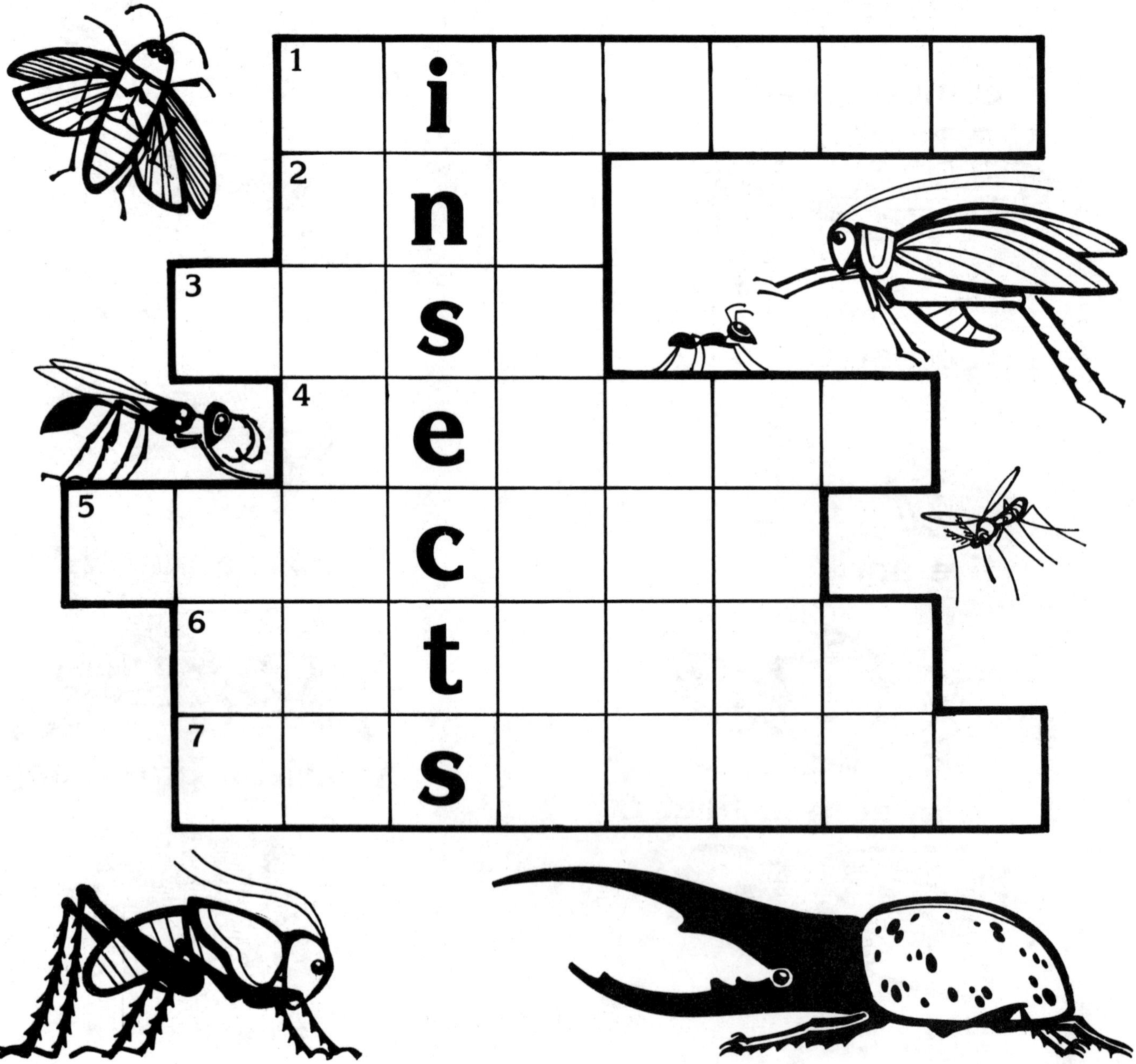

i n s e c t s

Name _____

ABC Beetles

Write the "first names" of these beetles on the lines in ABC order. Check off each beetle's name as you use it. The first one has been done for you.

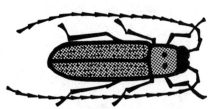

☐ **steel beetle**

☐ **long-horned beetle**

☐ **potato beetle**

☐ **water beetle**

1. <u>bean</u>

2. _____

3. _____

4. _____

5. _____

6. _____

7. _____

8. _____

9. _____

10. _____

☐ **giant beetle**

☒ **bean beetle**

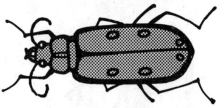

☐ **tiger beetle**

☐ **click beetle**

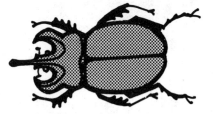

☐ **ox beetle**

☐ **unicorn beetle**

Where Do Insects Live?

Insects can be found almost anywhere! Here are some of the places insects live.

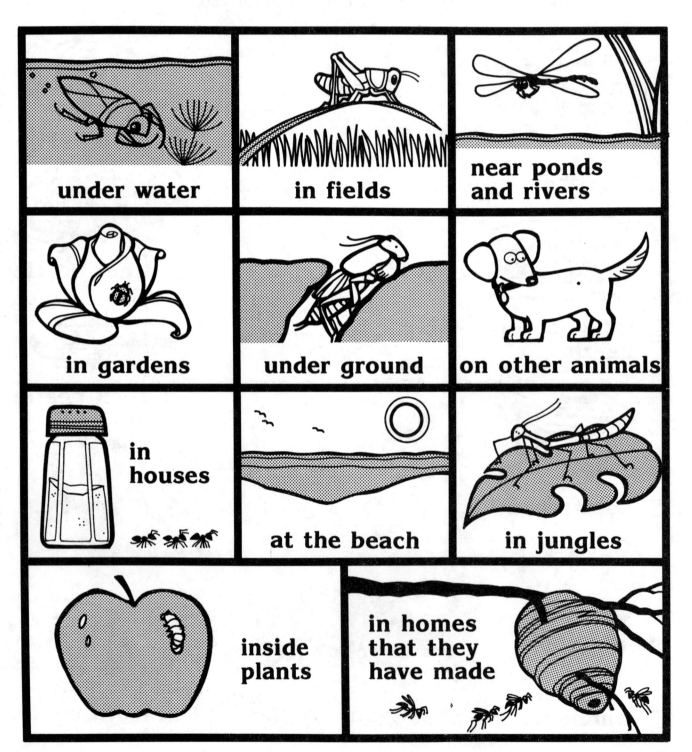

under water

in fields

near ponds and rivers

in gardens

under ground

on other animals

in houses

at the beach

in jungles

inside plants

in homes that they have made

Name _____

Where Do They Go?

Cut out the insects. Paste each one where it belongs.

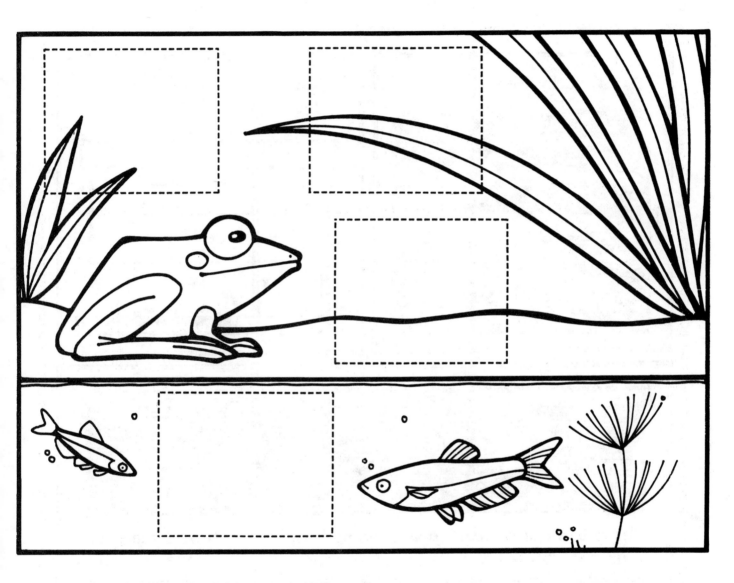

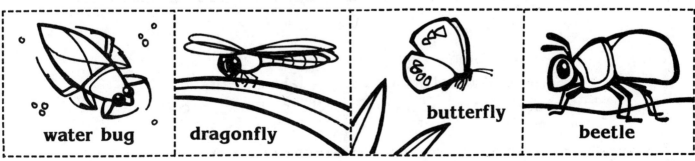

water bug **dragonfly** **butterfly** **beetle**

What Are Social Insects?

Social insects are insects that live together in large groups, or **colonies**. Ants, bees, and termites live in colonies. They work together to make a home.

Ants usually live underground.

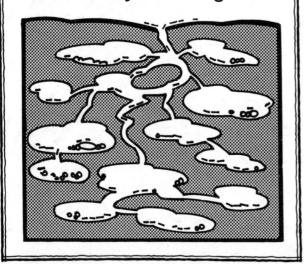

Bees may live in hives or in hollow trees.

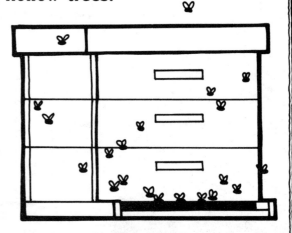

Termites live in trees, in wooden buildings, or in towers made of mud.

In a colony, each insect has a special job to do. Some insects collect food. Some take care of the baby insects. Other insects build or fix the home. A colony is like a tiny city.

Name _____

Termite Tower

Some termites in Africa build very tall nests of mud. Connect the dots to draw an African animal standing next to this termite nest.

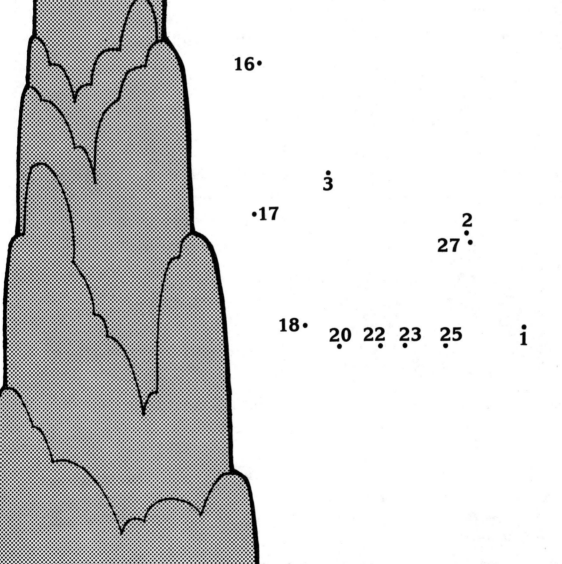

11. .9

12. . .8   7

10

13

5

14   6

.15

.4

16.

3.

.17

2

27

18. 20 22 23 25   1

19.   21.   .24   .26

How Do Insects Move?

Insects must move to get food and to run away from danger. Insects move in many different ways.

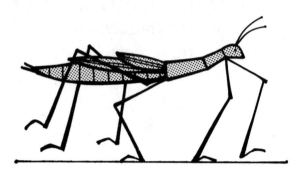

Some insects walk.

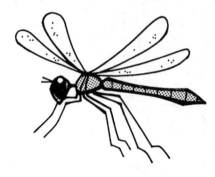

Many insects can fly.

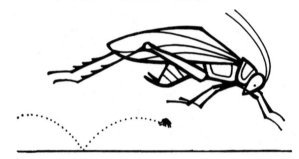

Crickets and fleas and katydids jump.

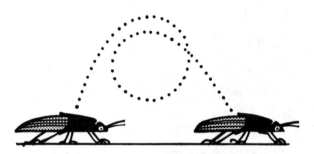

The click beetle can flip upside down when it jumps.

Some insects swim.

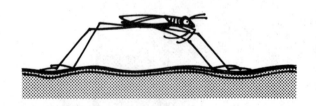

Some insects can walk on water!

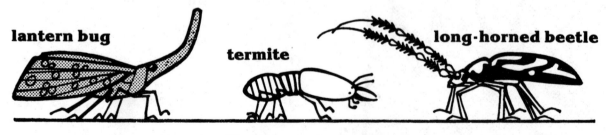

lantern bug **termite** **long-horned beetle**

Many insects crawl.

Name _____

Hop, Flip, Zip

Look at the letters in this box. Find and circle
eleven words that name ways insects can move.

```
H  O  P  Z  F  L  Y
J  C  L  I  M  B  C
U  R  S  P  E  A  R
M  A  W  A  L  K  E
P  W  I  G  G  L  E
Y  L  M  F  L  I  P
```

Word Box

climb • crawl • creep • flip • fly • hop
jump • swim • walk • wiggle • zip

Name _____

What Do Insects Eat?

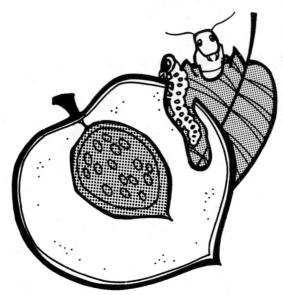

Many animals eat plant parts, such as leaves, fruit, wood, and seeds.

Some insects eat other insects, spiders, lizards, or baby fish.

Some insects eat dead animals or garbage.

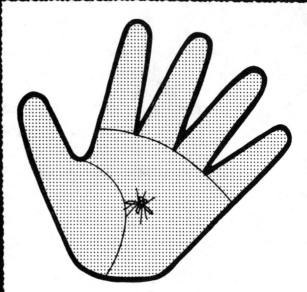

Mosquitoes and fleas drink a little blood when they bite other animals.

Name _____

Who Eats What?

Follow the dotted lines to connect each insect with its food.

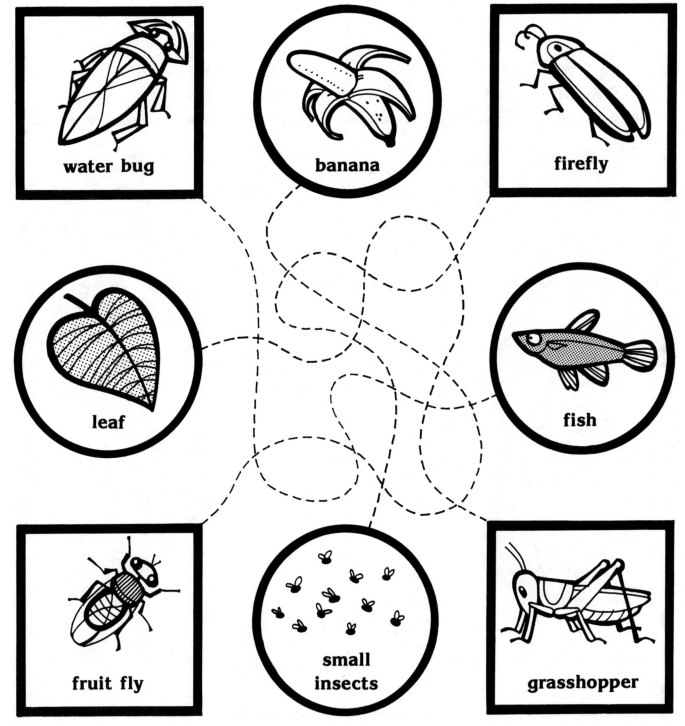

Which Animals Eat Insects?

Some small snakes eat
grasshoppers and crickets.

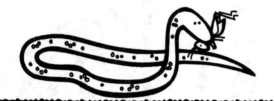

Insects are the food
of many spiders.

The chameleon uses its long tongue to catch insects.

Birds that eat insects
usually have small, thin beaks.

swallow

blackbird

wren

The archer fish
knocks insects into the water
by spitting on them.
Then it eats them.

Which Animals Eat Insects?
(continued)

The praying mantis is an insect that eats insects.

Sometimes, fish jump out of the water to eat insects.

trout

An anteater can eat 200 ants in one minute!

Frogs and toads are good insect catchers.

Helpful bats eat thousands of mosquitoes.

Name _____

Bugs for Lunch

Read pages 20 and 21 about animals that eat insects. Then look at the sentences below. Draw a line from each sentence to the word that is missing from that sentence.

1. Helpful _____ eat mosquitoes.

2. Birds that eat insects have thin _____.

3. An _____ can eat 200 ants in one minute.

4. The praying mantis is an _____ that eats insects.

5. The _____ fish spits water on insects.

6. The chameleon uses its _____ to catch insects.

7. Some small snakes eat _____ and crickets.

8. Frogs and _____ are good insect catchers.

A. insect

B. tongue

C. bats

D. beaks

E. archer

F. anteater

G. toads

H. grasshoppers

Name _____

Amazing Ant

Help the ant get away from the ant-eater by crawling through the maze.

How Do Insects Protect Themselves?

Ants, bees, and wasps can **sting**.

Grasshoppers can **jump** and **fly** away from their enemies.

Many caterpillars are covered with **spines**.

Water bugs **bite**.

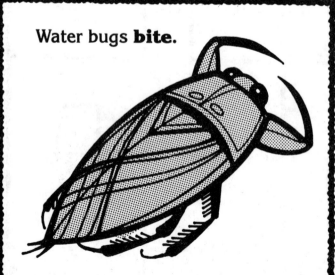

Monarch butterflies **taste bad**. Birds that eat them get sick.

How Do Insects Protect Themselves?
(continued)

The thorn bug **hides** by looking like part of a plant.

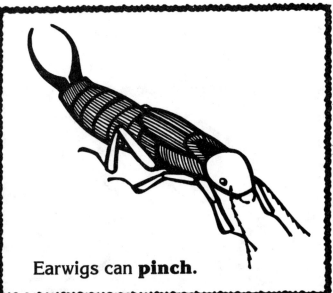

Earwigs can **pinch**.

Many beetles and other insects are protected by very **hard bodies**.

There are several kinds of stink bugs. They **smell bad**.

Some insects **scare** their enemies. This caterpillar has spots that look like a strange face.

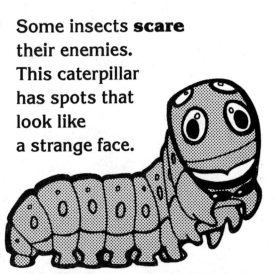

Name _____

Hidden Insects

Find the beetle, butterfly, caterpillar, fly, and walkingstick hidden in this garden. Color the picture.

Name _____

Bug Puzzle

leaf insect

This strange insect looks like leaves. It hides in bushes from animals that want to eat it. Cut the squares apart and arrange them to make a picture of a **leaf insect**.

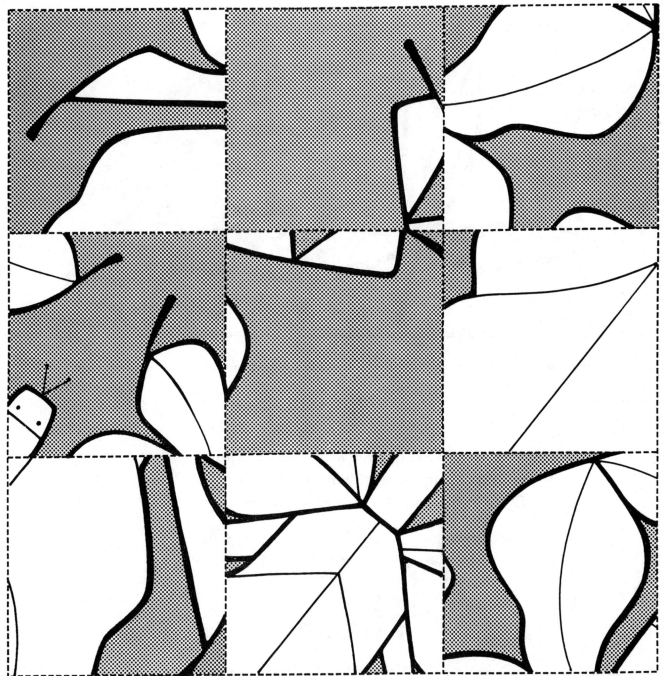

What Is Metamorphosis?

Metamorphosis (met-uh-MOR-fuh-sus) means change. This word is used to describe the way some insects change as they grow. Here are the four stages of **complete metamorphosis**.

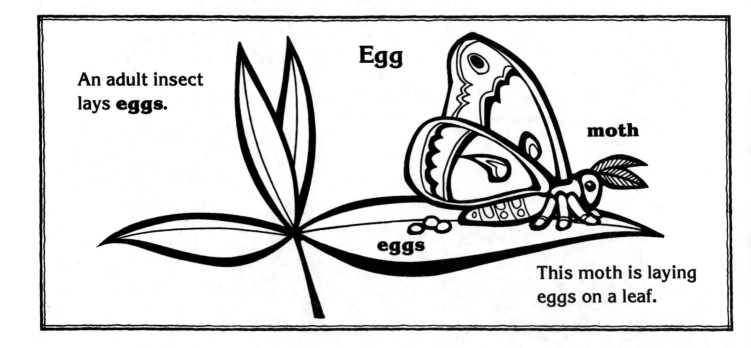

An adult insect lays **eggs**.

Egg

moth

eggs

This moth is laying eggs on a leaf.

Larva

The **larva** (LAWR-vuh) is a wormlike animal that hatches from an insect egg. A larva eats and grows. The larva of a butterfly or moth is called a **caterpillar**.

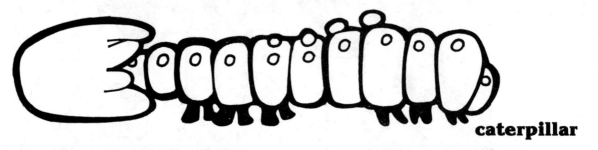

caterpillar

What Is Metamorphosis?
(continued)

Pupa

Later, the larva becomes a **pupa** (PEW-puh). The pupa has a hard skin. It does not eat or move around, but it changes in many ways. Slowly it turns into an adult insect. A caterpillar turns into a pupa when it is inside its cocoon.

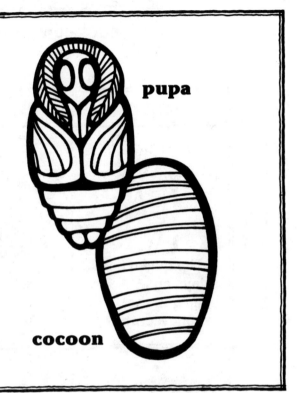

pupa

cocoon

Adult

When the pupa has turned into an **adult** insect, its hard skin cracks open. The adult insect crawls out.

Some of the insects that go through a **complete metamorphosis** are ants, wasps, flies, butterflies, and moths.

adult
insect

More Metamorphosis

Bees, beetles, and mosquitoes go through the four stages of **complete metamorphosis**.

	egg	larva	pupa	adult
bees	The queen bee lays an **egg** in the honeycomb.	The **larva** is fed by worker bees.	Worker bees seal the **pupa** in its hole.	A new **adult** bee crawls out of the hole.
beetles	Some beetles lay **eggs** in cereal, flour, or grain.	The beetle **larva** eats the food around it and grows.	The **pupa** does not eat.	The pupa becomes an **adult** beetle.
mosquitoes	Mosquito **eggs** float in water like a tiny boat.	The mosquito **larva** breathes through an air tube.	The **pupa** rests near the surface of the water.	The pupa's skin splits, and an **adult** mosquito comes out.

Other Ways Insects Grow

Not all insects go through a complete metamorphosis. Here are some other ways they grow.

silverfish

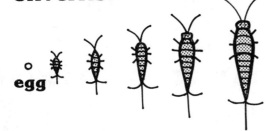

egg

The silverfish lays eggs. The eggs hatch into babies which look like the adults. The babies grow as they get older.

A few insects have eggs that hatch inside their bodies. The babies are then born alive.

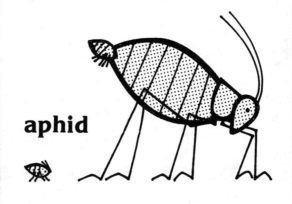

aphid

Grasshoppers and dragonflies go through **three** stages of **incomplete metamorphosis**: egg, **nymph**, and adult. Nymphs eat and grow. They look like adults but are not exactly like them. Many nymphs have very small wings or no wings at all.

grasshopper

dragonfly

eggs   nymph

eggs   nymph

adult

adult

Name _____

Caterpillar Words

More than one hundred words can be made from the letters in the word

caterpillar.

How many of these words can you find? Follow the game rules. Write your words on the lines below. If you need more space, use the back of this page or a separate sheet of paper.

Game Rules

1. Each word you write must have three or more letters.
2. You may use the letters in any order.
3. In any one word, you may use a letter only as often as it appears in the word **caterpillar**.

Example: You may write *pet*, but you may not write *pep*.

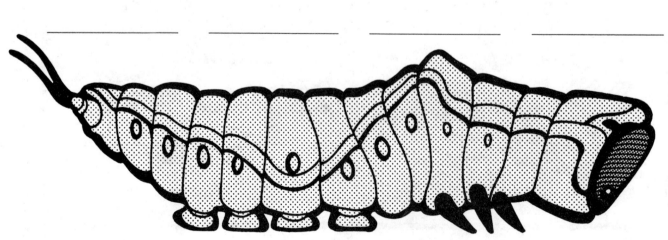

Following Directions
Letter Recognition
Color Matching

Color a Checkerspot

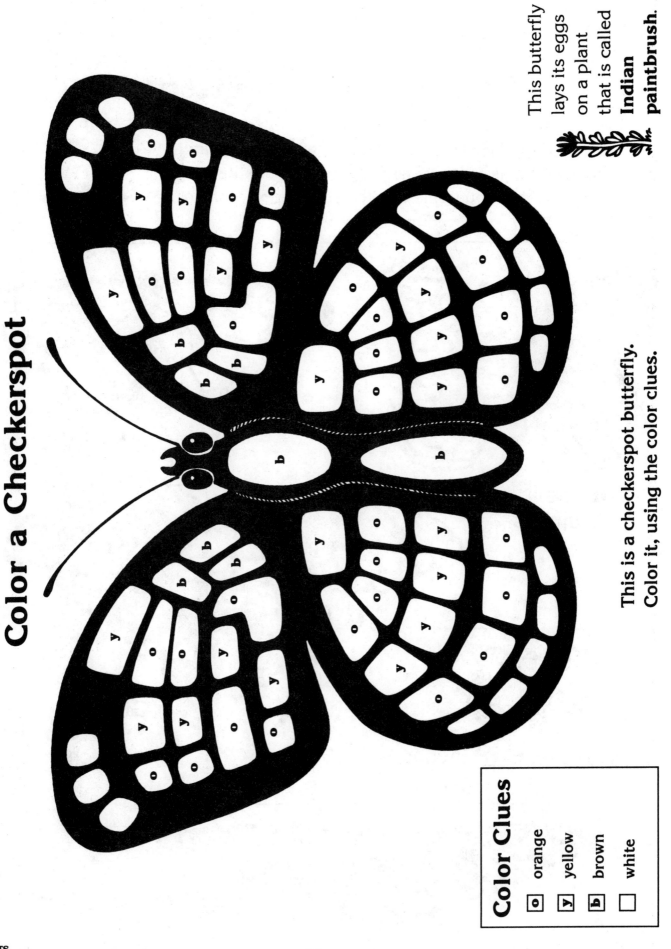

This butterfly
lays its eggs
on a plant
that is called
**Indian
paintbrush.**

This is a checkerspot butterfly.
Color it, using the color clues.

Color Clues

- **o** orange
- **y** yellow
- **b** brown
- ☐ white

Name _____

How Big Is the Butterfly?

The distance from one edge of a butterfly's wings to the other is called its **wingspan**. Measure the wingspans of these butterflies. Write a number on each line.

wingspan

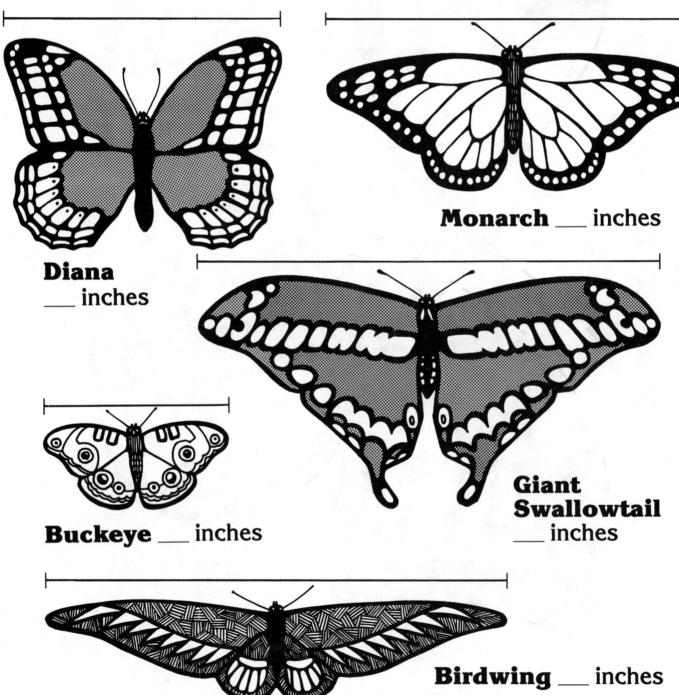

Diana
___ inches

Monarch ___ inches

Buckeye ___ inches

Giant Swallowtail
___ inches

Birdwing ___ inches

Name _____

More Measuring

Measure the wingspans of these butterflies. Write
a measurement on each line.

Zebra Longwing ___ inches

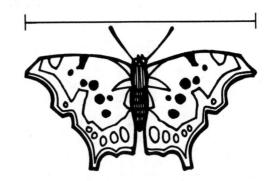

Question Mark ___ inches

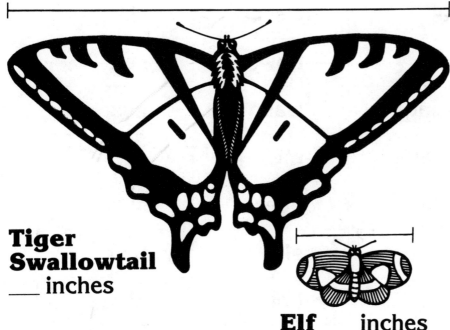

Tiger Swallowtail ___ inches

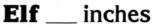

Elf ___ inches

Pixie ___ inches

Pine White ___ inches

Dogface ___ inches

Name _____

Rhyme Time

When words begin with different sounds but end with the same sound, we say they **rhyme**. The words *house* and *mouse* rhyme. Some words that end with the same letters do not rhyme. The words *hear* and *bear* do not rhyme. Some words that end with different letters do rhyme. The words *bird* and *word* do rhyme. In each row, circle the one word that rhymes with the first word.

1. ant	tiny	plant	any
2. crawl	tall	tree	climb
3. bee	leaf	flower	see
4. wing	sting	wasp	nest
5. flea	beetle	me	eat
6. honey	hive	bees	sunny
7. fly	flew	sky	fast
8. bug	dug	hole	hide
9. log	moth	leg	frog
10. cricket	tickle	ticket	take

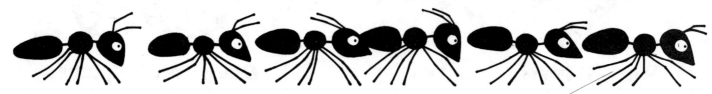

Name _____

Potato Bug Poetry

Write a poem about an insect on the lines below.
Use some of the words listed on page 36. In your poem,
tell why the insect is funny or pretty or unusual. Draw
a picture to go with your poem on a separate sheet
of paper. Cut out your poem. Paste your poem and
your picture on a larger sheet of paper.

Example

*A beetle looked up
at the sky
and waved her feelers
at a dragonfly.*

_____

_____

_____

_____

_____

_____

_____

Name _____

State Insects

The people in some states have chosen animals that are common or popular where they live to be symbols for their states. Here is a list of the animals chosen by people in two states.

Animals	States	
	Connecticut	**North Carolina**
state bird	robin	cardinal
state mammal	sperm whale	gray squirrel
state insect	praying mantis	honeybee

If you could choose any insect that lives in your state to be your "state insect," which one would you choose? Write the name of the insect on this line.

_____

Draw a picture of the insect you have chosen on the back of this page or on another sheet of paper.

Name _____

Insect Safari

Look for insects in a field, yard, park, or play-
ground. How many of these things can you find? Put
an **X** in the box beside each one that you see.

☐ an insect
that is flying

☐ an insect
that is sitting
on a plant

☐ an insect that is walking on the ground

☐ an insect
that is eating
or drinking

☐ three or more
insects together
in one place

☐ something that has been
partly eaten by an insect

an insect that is mostly

☐ red or orange

☐ green or blue

☐ brown or black

☐ an insect home

☐ a spider (which is not
an insect, but
eats insects)

Interesting Insects

Some stick insects have bodies thirteen inches long.

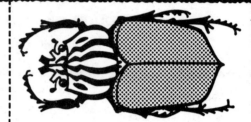

A Goliath beetle may weigh more than half a pound.

The sphinx moth has a tongue eleven inches long.

Some insects taste with their feet.

A honeybee beats its wings 15,000 times a minute when it is flying.

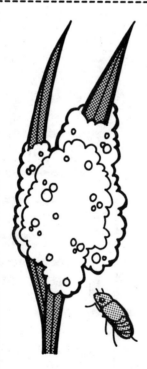

The froghopper hides in a nest of sticky bubbles.

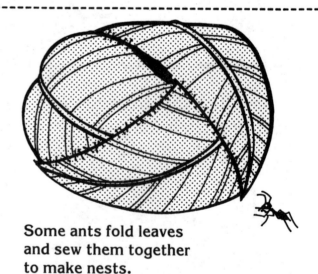

Some ants fold leaves and sew them together to make nests.

A queen termite may live more than fifty years.

Interesting Insects
(continued)

The potter wasp uses mud to make a nest that looks like a tiny clay pot.

Some moths can fly thirty miles per hour.

A grasshopper can jump twenty feet.

Diving beetles carry bubbles of air under their wing cases.

Some insects have feelers that are much longer than their bodies.

Migrating monarch butterflies sometimes fly as far as eighty miles in one day.

A cricket's "ears" are on its legs.

Adult mayflies live only one day. They have no mouths and do not eat.

Insect Quiz

Read these eight questions carefully. Put an **X** in the box beside each right answer. For some questions, you need to mark more than one box.

1. How many legs does an insect have?
   ☐ four   ☐ six   ☐ eight   ☐ ten

2. How many parts does an insect's body have?
   ☐ two   ☐ three   ☐ four   ☐ five

3. Which **two** of these animals are insects?
   ☐ worm   ☐ spider   ☐ fly   ☐ bee

4. What do we call a group of ants living together?
   ☐ class   ☐ colony   ☐ family   ☐ pack

5. Which **three** of these things do insects eat?
   ☐ fruit   ☐ garbage   ☐ metal   ☐ wood

6. Which **three** of these animals eat insects?
   ☐ bird   ☐ frog   ☐ horse   ☐ spider

7. Which insect protects itself by stinging?
   ☐ grasshopper ☐ butterfly   ☐ beetle   ☐ bee

8. What do we call the larva of a butterfly?
   ☐ katydid   ☐ caterpillar   ☐ cocoon   ☐ earthworm

Bug Club Banner

In the shape below, design a flag for a club for children who like learning about insects.

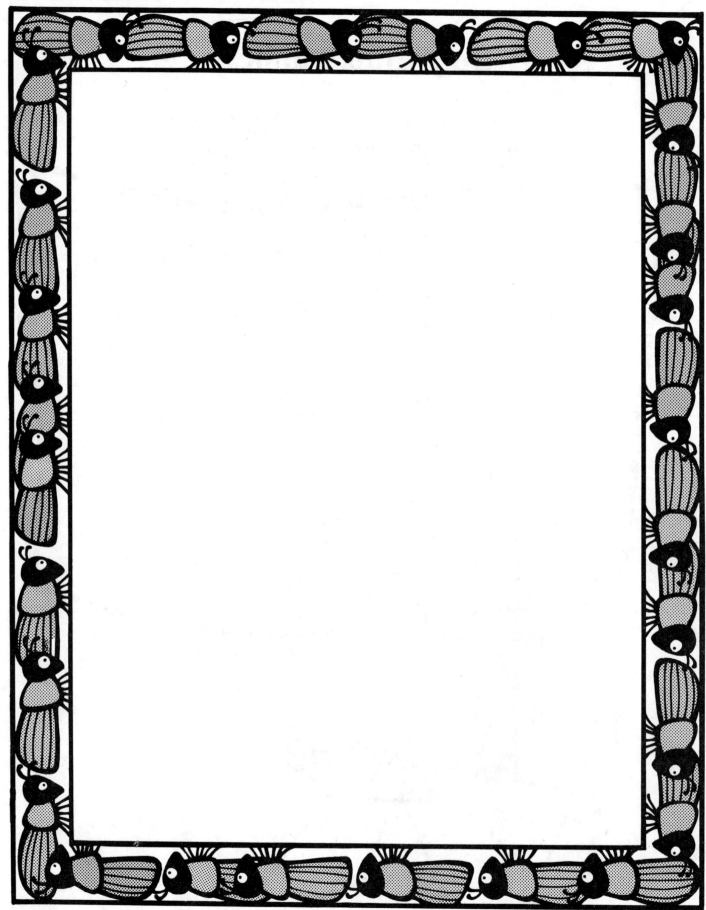

Beetle and Butterfly Borders

Ladybird Beetles

Cut from 4-inch-by-18-inch strips folded to be 4-inch-by-4½-inch rectangles. Use red or orange paper and add details with a black marking pen.

Butterflies

Cut from 4-inch-by-18-inch strips folded to be 4-inch-by-4½-inch rectangles. Use bright-colored paper and decorate if desired.

Awards

↑ name tag or note

button

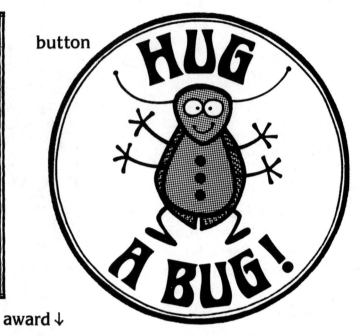

award ↓

_____
has learned about insects
and is now an official
INSECT INSPECTOR

Awarded by _____ on _____

Answer Key

Page 7, Which Ones Are Insects?
The horsefly, earwig, cabbage butterfly, and mosquito are insects.

Page 9, Connect the Insects
camel cricket–American grasshopper
red darter–ten-spot dragonfly
fire ant–potter wasp
long-horned beetle–steel beetle
tiger moth–buckeye butterfly

Page 10, Name Game
1. firefly
2. ant
3. wasp
4. beetle
5. cricket
6. katydid
7. mosquito

Page 11, ABC Beetles
1. bean
2. click
3. giant
4. long-horned
5. ox
6. potato
7. steel
8. tiger
9. unicorn
10. water

Page 13, Where Do They Go?

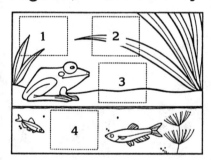

1. butterfly
2. dragonfly
3. beetle
4. water bug

Page 15, Termite Tower
The animal is a giraffe.

Page 17, Hop, Flip, Zip

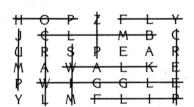

Page 19, Who Eats What?
water bug–fish
firefly–small insects
fruit fly–banana
grasshopper–leaf

Page 22, Bugs for Lunch
1. C
2. D
3. F
4. A
5. E
6. B
7. H
8. G

Page 23, Amazing Ant

Page 26, Hidden Insects

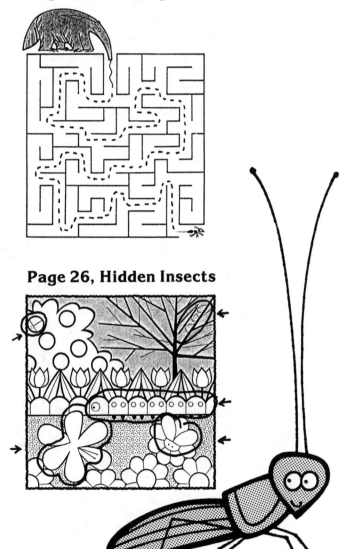

Answer Key
(continued)

Page 27, Bug Puzzle

Page 32, Caterpillar Words
Answers will vary, but possible words include act, air, apart, are, call, cap, care, carpet, ear, eat, ice, ill, lap, later, lie, lip, part, pile, place, price, race, rat, real, ripe, tail, tape, tear, and trace.

Page 34, How Big Is the Butterfly?
Monarch–4 inches
Diana–3 inches
Buckeye–2 inches
Giant Swallowtail–5 inches
Birdwing–5 inches

Page 35, More Measuring
Zebra Longwing–3½ inches
Question Mark–2½ inches
Tiger Swallowtail–4¾ inches
Pixie–1¾ inches
Pine White–1¾ inches
Elf–1¼ inches
Dogface–2¼ inches

Page 36, Rhyme Time
1. ant–plant
2. crawl–tall
3. bee–see
4. wing–sting
5. flea–me
6. honey–sunny
7. fly–sky
8. bug–dug
9. log–frog
10. cricket–ticket

Page 42, Insect Quiz
1. six
2. three
3. fly, bee
4. colony
5. fruit, garbage, wood
6. bird, frog, spider
7. bee
8. caterpillar

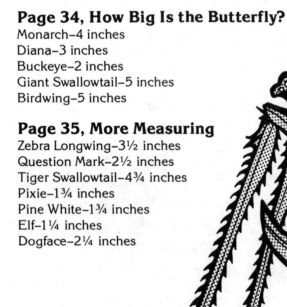

dead-leaf cricket